Pasta

Everyday recipes to enjoy

spaghetti & meatballs

ingredients

SERVES 2

2 thick slices white bread,
   crusts removed

2 tbsp olive oil

1 red onion, chopped

2 garlic cloves, finely
   chopped

400 g/14 oz canned chopped
   tomatoes

8 basil leaves

2 tbsp tomato purée

1 tsp sugar

salt and pepper

450 g/1 lb minced beef

2 eggs

1 tbsp chopped fresh parsley

1 tbsp chopped fresh basil

350 g/12 oz dried spaghetti

freshly grated Parmesan
   cheese, to serve

method

1 Place the bread in a shallow bowl and add just enough water to cover. Soak for 5 minutes, then drain and squeeze the bread to remove all the liquid.

2 Heat the oil in a saucepan, add the onion and half the garlic and cook over medium heat, stirring occasionally, for 5 minutes. Add the tomatoes with their juice, basil leaves, tomato purée and sugar and season with salt and pepper. Bring to the boil, reduce the heat and simmer, stirring occasionally, for 20 minutes until thickened and pulpy.

3 Mix the bread, beef, eggs, parsley, chopped basil, garlic and 1/2 tsp of salt by hand in a large mixing bowl. Roll small pieces of the meat mixture into balls. Drop the meatballs into the tomato sauce, cover the pan and cook over medium heat for 30 minutes.

4 Meanwhile, cook the spaghetti in a saucepan of lightly salted boiling water for 10 minutes, or until tender but still firm to the bite. Drain well.

5 Transfer the spaghetti to a large shallow serving bowl. Arrange the meatballs and sauce on top. Sprinkle 2 tablespoons of freshly grated Parmesan cheese over the top and serve with more cheese in a bowl on the side.

tagliatelle with a rich meat sauce

ingredients

SERVES 4

4 tbsp olive oil, plus extra
    for serving
85 g/3 oz pancetta or rindless
    lean bacon, diced
1 onion, chopped
1 garlic clove, chopped finely
1 carrot, chopped
1 celery stalk, chopped
225 g/8 oz minced steak
115 g/4 oz chicken livers,
    chopped
2 tbsp strained tomatoes
125 ml/4 fl oz dry white wine
250 ml/8 fl oz beef stock or
    water
1 tbsp chopped fresh oregano
1 bay leaf
salt and pepper
450 g/1 lb dried tagliatelle
freshly grated Parmesan
    cheese, to serve

method

1 Heat the olive oil in a large, heavy-bottom saucepan. Add the pancetta or bacon and cook over medium heat, stirring occasionally, for 3–5 minutes, until it is just turning brown. Add the onion, garlic, carrot and celery and cook, stirring occasionally, for a further 5 minutes.

2 Add the steak and cook over high heat, breaking up the meat with a wooden spoon, for 5 minutes, until browned. Stir in the chicken livers and cook, stirring occasionally, for a further 2–3 minutes. Add the strained tomatoes, wine, stock, oregano and bay leaf and season with salt and pepper. Bring to the boil, reduce the heat, cover and simmer for 30–35 minutes.

3 When the sauce is almost cooked, bring a large saucepan of lightly salted water to the boil. Add the pasta, bring back to the boil and cook for 8–10 minutes, until tender but still firm to the bite. Drain, transfer to a warmed serving dish, drizzle with a little olive oil and toss well.

4 Remove and discard the bay leaf from the sauce, then pour the sauce over the pasta, toss again and serve immediately with grated Parmesan cheese.

spaghetti alla carbonara

ingredients

SERVES 4

450 g/1 lb dried spaghetti

1 tbsp olive oil

225 g/8 oz rindless pancetta
    or lean bacon, chopped

4 eggs

5 tbsp single cream

salt and pepper

4 tbsp freshly grated
    Parmesan cheese

method

1 Bring a large, heavy-based saucepan of lightly salted water to the boil. Add the pasta, return to the boil and cook for 8–10 minutes, or until tender but still firm to the bite.

2 Meanwhile, heat the olive oil in a heavy-based frying pan. Add the chopped pancetta and cook over medium heat, stirring frequently, for 8–10 minutes.

3 Beat the eggs with the cream in a small bowl and season with salt and pepper. Drain the pasta and return it to the saucepan. Tip in the contents of the frying pan, then add the egg mixture and half the Parmesan cheese. Stir well, then transfer to a warmed serving dish. Serve immediately, sprinkled with the remaining Parmesan cheese.

rigatoni with ham, tomato & chilli sauce

ingredients

SERVES 4

1 tbsp olive oil

2 tbsp butter

1 onion, chopped finely

150 g/5½ oz ham, diced

2 garlic cloves, chopped
   very finely

1 fresh red chilli, deseeded
   and chopped finely

800 g/1 lb 12 oz canned
   chopped tomatoes

salt and pepper

450 g/1 lb rigatoni or penne

2 tbsp chopped fresh flat-leaf
   parsley

6 tbsp freshly grated
   Parmesan cheese

method

1 Put the olive oil and 1 tablespoon of the butter in a large saucepan over medium–low heat. Add the onion and fry for 10 minutes until soft and golden. Add the ham and fry for 5 minutes until lightly browned. Stir in the garlic, chilli and tomatoes. Season with a little salt and pepper. Bring to the boil, then simmer over medium-low heat for 30–40 minutes until thickened.

2 Cook the pasta in plenty of boiling salted water until tender but still firm to the bite. Drain and transfer to a warmed serving dish.

3 Pour the sauce over the pasta. Add the parsley, Parmesan cheese and the remaining butter. Toss well to mix and serve immediately.

chicken with basil & pine nut pesto

ingredients

SERVES 4

2 tbsp vegetable oil

4 skinless, boneless
    chicken breasts

350 g/12 oz dried farfalle

salt and pepper

sprig of fresh basil, to garnish

pesto

100 g/3½ oz shredded
    fresh basil

125 ml/4 fl oz extra virgin
    olive oil

3 tbsp pine nuts

3 garlic cloves, minced

55 g/2 oz freshly grated
    Parmesan cheese

2 tbsp freshly grated
    romano cheese

salt

method

1 To make the pesto, place the basil, olive oil, pine nuts, garlic and a generous pinch of salt in a food processor or blender and process until smooth. Scrape the mixture into a bowl and stir in the cheeses.

2 Heat the vegetable oil in a frying pan over medium heat. Fry the chicken breasts, turning once, for 8–10 minutes, or until the juices are no longer pink. Cut into small cubes.

3 Cook the pasta in plenty of lightly salted boiling water until tender but still firm to the bite. Drain and transfer to a warmed serving dish. Add the chicken and pesto, then season with pepper. Toss well to mix.

4 Garnish with a basil sprig and serve warm.

tagliatelle with creamy chicken & shiitake sauce

ingredients

SERVES 4

25 g/1 oz dried shiitake
    mushrooms
350 ml/12 fl oz hot water
1 tbsp olive oil
6 bacon slices, chopped
3 boneless, skinless chicken
    breasts, sliced into strips
115 g/4 oz fresh shiitake
    mushrooms, sliced
1 small onion, chopped finely
1 tsp fresh oregano or
    marjoram, chopped finely
275 ml/9 fl oz chicken stock
300 ml/10 fl oz double cream
salt and pepper
450 g/1 lb dried tagliatelle
55 g/2 oz freshly grated
    Parmesan cheese
chopped fresh flat-leaf
    parsley, to garnish

method

1 Put the dried mushrooms in a bowl with the hot water and soak for 30 minutes, or until softened. Remove, squeezing excess water back into the bowl. Strain the liquid through a fine-meshed sieve and reserve. Slice the soaked mushrooms, discarding the stems.

2 Heat the oil in a large frying pan over medium heat. Add the bacon and chicken, then stir-fry for about 3 minutes. Add the dried and fresh mushrooms, onion and oregano. Stir-fry for 5–7 minutes, or until soft. Pour in the stock and the mushroom liquid. Bring to the boil, stirring. Simmer for about 10 minutes, continuing to stir, until reduced. Add the cream and simmer for 5 minutes, stirring, until beginning to thicken. Season with salt and pepper. Remove the pan from the heat and set aside.

3 Cook the pasta until tender but still firm to the bite. Drain and transfer to a serving dish. Pour the sauce over the pasta. Add half the Parmesan cheese and mix. Sprinkle with parsley and serve with the remaining Parmesan cheese.

linguine alla puttanesca

ingredients

SERVES 4

450 g/1 lb plum tomatoes
3 tbsp olive oil
2 garlic cloves, finely
   chopped
10 anchovy fillets, drained
   and chopped
140 g/5 oz black olives, pitted
   and chopped
1 tbsp capers, rinsed
pinch of cayenne pepper
400 g/14 oz dried linguine
salt
2 tbsp chopped fresh flat-leaf
   parsley, to garnish
crusty bread, to serve

method

1 Peel the tomatoes by cutting a cross in the bottom of each and placing in a heatproof bowl. Cover with boiling water and let stand for 35–45 seconds. Drain and plunge into cold water, then the skins will slide off easily. Deseed and chop the tomatoes.

2 Heat the olive oil in a heavy-based saucepan. Add the garlic and cook over low heat, stirring frequently, for 2 minutes. Add the anchovies and mash them to a pulp with a fork. Add the olives, capers and tomatoes and season with cayenne pepper. Cover and simmer for 25 minutes.

3 Meanwhile, bring a saucepan of lightly salted water to the boil. Add the pasta, return to the boil and cook for 8–10 minutes, or until tender but still firm to the bite. Drain and transfer to a warmed serving dish.

4 Spoon the anchovy sauce into the dish and toss the pasta, using 2 large forks. Garnish with the parsley and serve immediately with crusty bread.

spaghetti with clams

ingredients

SERVES 4

1 kg/2 lb 4 oz live clams,
    scrubbed under cold
    running water*

175 ml/6 fl oz water

175 ml/6 fl oz dry white wine

350 g/12 oz dried spaghetti

5 tbsp olive oil

2 garlic cloves, finely
    chopped

4 tbsp chopped fresh
    flat-leaf parsley

salt and pepper

* discard any clams with
    broken or damaged shells
    and any that do not shut
    when sharply tapped

method

1 Place the clams in a large, heavy-based saucepan, add the water and wine, cover and cook over high heat, shaking the pan occasionally, for 5 minutes, or until the shells have opened.

2 Remove the clams with a slotted spoon and cool slightly. Strain the cooking liquid, through a sieve lined with cheesecloth, into a small pan. Bring to the boil and cook until reduced by about half, then remove from the heat. Meanwhile, discard any clams that have not opened, remove the remainder from their shells and reserve until required.

3 Bring a large saucepan of lightly salted water to the boil. Add the pasta, return to the boil and cook for 8–10 minutes, or until tender but still firm to the bite.

4 Meanwhile, heat the olive oil in a large, heavy-based frying pan. Add the garlic and cook, stirring frequently, for 2 minutes. Add the parsley and the reduced clam cooking liquid and simmer gently.

5 Drain the pasta and add it to the frying pan with the clams. Season with salt and pepper and cook, stirring constantly, for 4 minutes, or until the pasta is coated and the clams have heated through. Transfer to a warmed serving dish and serve immediately.

spaghetti with prawns & garlic sauce

ingredients

SERVES 4

3 tbsp olive oil

3 tbsp butter

4 garlic cloves, minced

2 tbsp finely diced red
    pepper

2 tbsp tomato purée

125 ml/4 fl oz dry white wine

450 g/1 lb spaghetti or
    tagliatelle

350 g/12 oz raw shelled
    prawns

125 ml/4 fl oz double cream

salt and pepper

3 tbsp chopped fresh flat-leaf
    parsley, to garnish

method

1 Heat the oil and butter in a saucepan over medium–low heat. Add the garlic and red pepper. Fry for a few seconds until the garlic is just beginning to colour. Stir in the tomato purée and wine. Cook for 10 minutes, stirring.

2 Cook the spaghetti in plenty of boiling salted water until tender but still firm to the bite. Drain and return to the saucepan.

3 Add the prawns to the sauce and raise the heat to medium–high. Cook for 2 minutes, stirring, until the prawns turn pink. Reduce the heat and stir in the cream. Cook for 1 minute, stirring constantly, until thickened. Season with salt and pepper.

4 Transfer the spaghetti to a warmed serving dish and pour over the sauce. Sprinkle with the parsley. Toss well to mix and serve at once.

spaghetti with tomato, garlic & basil sauce

ingredients

SERVES 4

5 tbsp extra virgin olive oil

1 onion, chopped finely

800 g/1 lb 12 oz canned
    chopped tomatoes

4 garlic cloves, cut into
    quarters

salt and pepper

450 g/1 lb dried spaghetti

large handful fresh basil
    leaves, shredded

fresh Parmesan cheese
    shavings, to serve

method

1 Heat the oil in a large saucepan over medium heat. Add the onion and fry gently for 5 minutes until soft. Add the tomatoes and garlic. Bring to the boil, then simmer over medium–low heat for 25–30 minutes until the oil separates from the tomato. Season with salt and pepper.

2 Cook the pasta in plenty of boiling salted water until tender but still firm to the bite. Drain and transfer to a warmed serving dish.

3 Pour the sauce over the pasta. Add the basil and toss well to mix. Serve with the Parmesan cheese shavings.

aubergines & pasta

ingredients

SERVES 4

150 ml/5 fl oz vegetable stock

150 ml/5 fl oz white wine
  vinegar

2 tsp balsamic vinegar

3 tbsp olive oil

1 fresh oregano sprig

450 g/1 lb aubergines, peeled
  and thinly sliced

400 g/14 oz dried linguine

marinade

2 tbsp extra virgin olive oil

2 garlic cloves, crushed

2 tbsp chopped fresh oregano

2 tbsp finely chopped roasted
  almonds

2 tbsp diced red pepper

2 tbsp lime juice

grated rind and juice
  of 1 orange

salt and pepper

method

1 Place the vegetable stock, wine vinegar and balsamic vinegar into a large, heavy-based saucepan and bring to the boil over low heat. Add 2 teaspoons of the olive oil and the oregano sprig, and simmer gently for 1 minute. Add the aubergine slices to the pan, remove from the heat and let stand for 10 minutes.

2 Meanwhile, make the marinade. Mix the olive oil, garlic, fresh oregano, almonds, pepper, lime juice and orange rind and juice together in a large bowl, and season with salt and pepper.

3 Carefully remove the aubergine from the pan with a slotted spoon, and drain well. Add the aubergine slices to the marinade, mixing well, and let marinate in the refrigerator for 12 hours.

4 Bring a large, heavy-based saucepan of lightly salted water to the boil. Add half of the remaining olive oil and the linguine, return to the boil and cook for 8–10 minutes, or until just tender but still firm to the bite. Drain the pasta thoroughly and toss with the remaining olive oil while still warm. Arrange the pasta on a serving plate with the aubergine slices and the marinade. Serve immediately.

penne in a creamy mushroom sauce

ingredients

SERVES 4

55 g/2 oz butter

1 tbsp olive oil

6 shallots, sliced

450 g/1 lb chestnut
mushrooms, sliced

salt and pepper

1 tsp plain flour

150 ml/5 fl oz double cream

2 tbsp port

115 g/4 oz sun-dried
tomatoes in oil, drained
and chopped

pinch freshly grated nutmeg

350 g/12 oz dried penne

2 tbsp chopped fresh flat-leaf
parsley, to garnish

method

1 Melt the butter with the olive oil in a large, heavy-based frying pan. Add the shallots and cook over low heat, stirring occasionally, for 4–5 minutes, or until softened. Add the mushrooms and cook over low heat for a further 2 minutes. Season with salt and pepper, sprinkle in the flour and cook, stirring, for 1 minute.

2 Remove the pan from the heat and gradually stir in the cream and port. Return to the heat, add the sun-dried tomatoes and grated nutmeg and cook over low heat, stirring occasionally, for 8 minutes.

3 Meanwhile, bring a large, heavy-based saucepan of lightly salted water to the boil. Add the pasta, return to the boil and cook for 8–10 minutes, or until tender but still firm to the bite. Drain the pasta well and add to the mushroom sauce. Cook for 3 minutes, then transfer to a warmed serving dish. Sprinkle with the chopped parsley and serve immediately.

tagliatelle with asparagus & gorgonzola sauce

ingredients

SERVES 4

450 g/1 lb asparagus tips
olive oil
salt and pepper
225 g/8 oz Gorgonzola,
	crumbled
175 ml/6 fl oz double cream
350 g/12 oz dried tagliatelle

method

1 Place the asparagus tips in a single layer in a shallow ovenproof dish. Sprinkle with a little olive oil and season with salt and pepper. Turn to coat in the oil and seasoning. Roast in a preheated oven, 230°C/450°F/Gas Mark 8, for 10–12 minutes, until slightly browned and just tender. Set aside and keep warm.

2 Combine the crumbled cheese with the cream in a bowl. Season with salt and pepper.

3 Cook the pasta in plenty of boiling salted water until tender but still firm to the bite. Drain and transfer to a warmed serving dish.

4 Immediately add the asparagus and the cheese mixture. Toss well until the cheese has melted and the pasta is coated with the sauce. Serve at once.

farfalle with cream & parmesan

ingredients

SERVES 4

450 g/1 lb dried farfalle

2 tbsp unsalted butter

350 g/12 oz petits pois

200 ml/7 fl oz double cream

pinch of freshly grated
nutmeg

salt and pepper

55 g/2 oz freshly grated
Parmesan cheese,
plus extra to serve

fresh flat-leaf parsley sprigs,
to garnish

crusty bread, to serve

method

1 Bring a large saucepan of lightly salted water to the boil. Add the pasta, return to the boil and cook for 8–10 minutes, or until tender but still firm to the bite, then drain thoroughly.

2 Melt the butter in a large, heavy-based saucepan. Add the petits pois and cook for 2–3 minutes. Add 150 ml/5 fl oz of the cream and bring to the boil. Reduce the heat and simmer for 1 minute, or until slightly thickened.

3 Add the drained pasta to the cream mixture. Place the pan over low heat and toss until the farfalle are thoroughly coated. Season with nutmeg, salt and pepper, then add the remaining cream and the grated Parmesan cheese. Toss again and transfer to individual serving bowls. Garnish with parsley sprigs and serve immediately with extra Parmesan cheese, for sprinkling, and crusty bread.

fettuccine with ricotta

ingredients

SERVES 4

350 g/12 oz dried fettuccine

3 tbsp unsalted butter

2 tbsp chopped fresh flat-leaf
 parsley, plus extra leaves
 to garnish

225 g/8 oz ricotta cheese

225 g/8 oz ground almonds

150 ml/5 fl oz soured cream

2 tbsp extra virgin olive oil

125 ml/4 fl oz hot chicken
 stock

pinch of freshly grated nutmeg

salt and pepper

1 tbsp pine nuts

method

1 Bring a large heavy-based saucepan of lightly salted water to the boil. Add the pasta, return to the boil and cook for 8–10 minutes, or until tender but still firm to the bite. Drain well and return to the pan. Add the butter and chopped parsley and toss thoroughly to coat.

2 Mix the ricotta, ground almonds and soured cream together in a bowl. Gradually stir in the olive oil, followed by the hot chicken stock. Season with nutmeg and pepper.

3 Transfer the pasta to a warmed dish, pour over the sauce and toss. Sprinkle with pine nuts, garnish with parsley leaves and serve immediately.

This edition published by Parragon Books Ltd in 2013
LOVE FOOD is an imprint of Parragon Books Ltd

Parragon Books Ltd
Chartist House
15–17 Trim Street
Bath BA1 1HA, UK
www.parragon.com/lovefood

ISBN 978-1-4723-2235-7

Printed in China

Notes for the Reader
This book uses both metric and imperial measurements. Follow the same units of measurement throughout; do not mix metric and imperial. All spoon measurements are level: teaspoons are assumed to be 5 ml, and tablespoons are assumed to be 15 ml. Unless otherwise stated, milk is assumed to be full fat, eggs and individual vegetables are medium, and pepper is freshly ground black pepper. Unless otherwise stated, all root vegetables should be washed in plain water and peeled prior to using.

For best results, use a food thermometer when cooking meat and poultry – check the latest government guidelines for current advice.

Garnishes, decorations and serving suggestions are all optional and not necessarily included in the recipe ingredients or method.

The times given are an approximate guide only. Preparation times differ according to the techniques used by different people and the cooking times may also vary from those given. Optional ingredients, variations or serving suggestions have not been included in the time calculations.

Recipes using raw or very lightly cooked eggs should be avoided by infants, the elderly, pregnant women, convalescents and anyone suffering from an illness. Pregnant and breastfeeding women are advised to avoid eating peanuts and peanut products. Sufferers from nut allergies should be aware that some of the ready-made ingredients used in the recipes in this book may contain nuts. Always check the packaging before use.